Write Something

By Mitch Levenberg

Write Something

By Mitch Levenberg

Irene Weinberger Books
an imprint of Hamilton Stone Editions

Maplewood, New Jersey

ISBN 978-0-9836668-9-9
Library of Congress Cataloging-in-Publication Data
Levenberg, Mitch, 1952-
[Essays. Selections]
Write Something / by Mitch Levenberg.
pages cm
ISBN 978-0-9836668-9-9
1. Creation (Literary, artistic, etc.) 2. Authorship. I. Title.
PS3612.E92336A6 2015
814'.6--dc23
2014049909

Printed in the United States of America
First Paper Printing 2015

Irene Weinberger Books/Hamilton Stone Editions
P.O. Box 43, Maplewood, NJ 07040
Ireneweinbergerbooks.com

Cover art by Jeremy Busch

Also by Mitch Levenberg

Principles of Uncertainty and Other Constants

Acknowledgements

To **Jeremy Busch**-my blogicist-for creating both the title and cover art for this book as well as for his continual encouragement and great ideas.

To **Kat Chua Almiranez**, **Nayanda Nikki Monique**, **Penina Roth**, **Christina Vines**, **David Oliver** and **Roberta Bonisson** and all those who have given me the opportunity to read my work

To my Reading and Writing friends and partners **Marilynn Lundy**, **Annette Lieberman**, **Jason Dubow**, **Gregory Tague**, **Ellen Press-Scott**, all the great writers and readers of my seniors writing class, and most of all my wife **Julie**, who help and inspire me to write and who tell me about all the great books I still need to read.

To my late parents, my grandmother, Abraham Lincoln, Mr. Spock, C.C. Sabathia, Flushing Queens, Coconut Creek, Florida, The Lower East Side of Manhattan, and other people and places that have given me the ideas and inspiration for the stories and essays in this collection.

Preface

Write Something is a collection of short essays which over the last few years have appeared as posts for my blog at MitchLevenberg.com or more endearingly known, perhaps, as the Mind of Mitch Levenberg. "Oh my God, I thought," writes Deborah Clearman, "what would it be like to be in the mind of Mitch Levenberg?" Many of these essays deal with the readings I've done at various locations in Brooklyn and Manhattan and discuss not just the readings themselves but the way I thought about these readings, about what I read, to whom I read, how I felt about what I read, and how I read what I read, and would I ever read what I read, and where I read what I read — again. They also deal with writing, my own writing process and the things and people in my life both chronic and sudden those things and people who remain, who linger on, and those who suddenly appear and then disappear just as suddenly but always leave a story behind to write about. But believe me, I wouldn't write a word unless I felt that you too would enjoy reading these stories as much as I did writing them. So. . .enjoy

Mitch Levenberg
Dec. 17, 2013

Table of Contents

Chapter 1

THINK COFFEE

I'm not here 10 minutes and I already love this place called Think Coffee. I always think coffee. First I think, "Am I still breathing?"and then I think coffee. Not always in that order. I was hungry and thirsty and the first thing I see on the chalkboard is a grilled cheese sandwich. When am I not in the mood for a grilled cheese sandwich? It's one of those nights where no one has even read yet but still I've thoroughly enjoyed the reading. You know what I mean? Take the restroom. You need a key to open it. The key is attached to a plastic cup next to the cash register. For a fleeting moment I think they might also want a urine sample. If this were the late sixties or early seventies, I probably would have been drunk or stoned enough to give them one. The bathroom walls are full of graffiti; well thought out graffiti, nothing chaotic or unwelcoming, no giant phallic drawings or comments on the bad service; there is a poem on the wall that reads, "Like a pallbearer of sense/NYC smells like embalming fluid/as we wake up legs entwined/two fresh corpses of pleasure." Wacky, cloying, over the top, under the bottom, pretentious, endearing, sexless, too much metaphor, deadly funny, hysterically serious, definitely in the category of things to read while peeing.

The theme for the reading tonight is "jobs." I wrote, quite accidentally or incidentally, about a job I never had, nor ever would have. I have nothing against bus drivers. I have always admired bus drivers but I could never be one, not in my wildest dreams. I have enough trouble driving a car. The story is kind of surreal. It's a bus to nowhere. It's about writing. It's about having to navigate a story when you have no idea where it's going, whether it might end up at a very satisfactory destination or go straight off a cliff. There are ghosts too. Plenty of ghosts. Sometimes you run them over, sometimes you don't. But they're always there.

Most people wrote about actual jobs they had. I could have written about a job I once had. I was a messenger on the 82nd floor of the World Trade Center. That was the summer of '76. It was a hot couple of days in July and I wore saddle shoes with two inch heels and a leisure suit. It was the summer of the Bicentennial and the Democratic National Convention at Madison Square Garden. I was sent by a temporary employment agency and I remember coming into the office and there were two guys and they had no idea what to do with me. One guy asked me to plug in a calculator. The outlet was under the table. I went under the table with my saddle shoes and my leisure suit and couldn't for the life of me figure out how to plug that thing into the outlet. I remember staying under the table for a long time too embarrassed to come out again. "Look at me," I thought to myself. "I'm a college graduate for God's sake." When I came back out from under the table with the plug still in my hand, one of the guys turned to the other and said,

"Did we throw the garbage out yet?"

Later some little old guy named Sandy showed up and said I was supposed to be a messenger so I rode up and down those supersonic elevators all day and delivered things to really raunchy offices where beefy sweaty guys with sauce stains on their shirts and playboy calendars with those same stains on them — hanging on the wall right behind the desks — and I'll never forget the playmate for the month of July wearing one of those tri-cornered Valley Forge hats and nothing else. I walked miles that day and the next day and at the end of the following day when they asked me why I didn't take the subway, I quit. Anyway, I could have told that story but I'm glad I didn't.

This is mostly because everyone else did. Not my story, of course, but stories about their own strange misadventures at various thankless jobs. One woman wrote about every bad job she ever had, a lifetime of bad jobs, it seemed until she finally took "early retirement." That seemed to be after about 50 years of working. When she sat down again, I told her that I remembered Patricia Murphy's, a restaurant she had mentioned in her piece and she said, looking at me with her gluten free eyes, "Yes, you look around the same age as I do." I was really upbeat until she said that. My bouncy heart that was falling in love with all those young female writers around me sunk to the ground. "Then those really are age spots I've been getting," I thought. Suddenly, I imagined myself smelling of formaldehyde. I was old again. "I better face it," I thought. If I wanted to feel young again I better stop going to Readings at East Village coffee houses and stick to A.A.R.P or nursing home events only. Then, rather than Think Coffee, I began to Think Maalox as that Grilled Cheese sandwich started to, as my mother would say, "repeat on me."

By the time I am introduced and begin to read my story, I am feeling a lot better. My heartburn is gone. I am feeling young again or perhaps so old people listen to me as they might listen to wind through trees, or the hoot of an unseen owl, or to a quiet argument between two people in a restaurant — where to hear them better you have to tilt your head just a fraction of an inch in their direction. I am the ghost of Walt Whitman, of Franz Kafka, of the man or woman who wrote that poem on the bathroom wall, and I never feel more alive.

Chapter 2

A LUCKY MAN

One morning, while visiting my mother in Florida, I found myself in Publix — the kind of supermarket we used to fantasize about back home — waiting on line for a lottery ticket. My mother was at the check-out counter waiting to pay for her groceries and asked me to get her a fantasy five ticket. When she said "fantasy five" it reminded me of my own family when I was growing up in Flushing — my brother, my mother and father, my grandmother and I — the fantasy five — all of us living in our own fantasy world. We weren't poor. After all, we had plenty of food and two TV sets and even a credit card — which belonged to my father. We also had a big crystal chandelier which hung precariously from the ceiling and had five light bulbs on it which sometimes burned all day and into the night whether they had to or not. My grandmother didn't like this — she thought we were wasting electricity. "That's five lights you're burning," she would tell us when no one was in the room. "Why do you need to burn five lights when there is no one in the room?"

This was the fear she lived with. The rest of us believed in the fantasy of getting rich, of having a bigger house in the suburbs — my grandmother's fantasy was much simpler — the fantasy of nothing ever going wrong — the fantasy that we would could always pay the electric bill — the fantasy that maybe if we never asked for much, if we never ventured too far from home — we would never have to die.

So there I was on line waiting for a single fantasy five ticket — total cost one dollar — and in front of me was a little old man — whose name was Lenny — with a stack of twenties in his hand buying more lottery tickets than I had ever seen anyone buy before — tickets of all different sizes and shapes and textures, tickets with pictures of flamingos and palm trees — was that a naked woman I saw? — the very stuff of fantasy.

There were so many tickets just spitting out of the machine, the woman behind the counter decided to leave for a while — she seemed to know this man — she seemed to know how long this fantasy transaction usually took. Ordinarily, I would have left the line, but the whole thing fascinated me.

"Do you ever win?" I asked Lenny.

"Sometimes," he said, but not the big one. Not yet — but I know someday I will."

"Why?" I asked. "Because you buy so many?"

"No," he said, "because I'm a lucky man. After all, I survived the Battle of the Bulge. Not too many people survived the Battle of the Bulge," he said. "I was one of the lucky ones."

Then he started to tell me about all those eighteen year olds, all those kids wet behind the ears who just graduated from high school — just wiped out — a whole generation of eighteen year olds wiped out at the Battle of the Bulge and somehow he survived. "Now I'm 91 years old," he said, "and I'm a very lucky man."

The whole time he was telling me this, his tickets just kept spitting out of the machine, some of them dropping onto the counter, some of them falling on the floor — the lottery woman still gone — no one keeping an eye on those tickets except for Lenny himself.

"Look at that," he said. She always walks away and I got to catch them, make sure I don't lose any. I've lost some before you know."

"You have?" I asked quite solemnly, not feeling anymore that I was talking about lottery tickets but instead about those eighteen year olds Lenny was talking about before — a whole generation of them just being spit out like those tickets in the machine, the unlucky ones, spit out of the war machine — almost 90,000 killed or wounded — and then this man who watched so many of them die — who could not save them, while he, somehow — by the luck of some eternal draw — got away without a scratch himself — a walking winning lottery ticket.

Lenny was not just a lucky man, but a hoarder of luck, a man addicted to luck. Luck had saved his life, would make him rich, would help him live to 100. He looked luck in the face and dared it for more. He craved it. He needed it. He tried to buy it. He would corner all the luck in the world if he could, but for now he would have to settle for a lottery counter at a Publix supermarket in Coconut Creek, Florida.

Lenny had an intimacy, an obsession with luck, neither I nor my mother, who at the age of 90, still fantasizing about becoming rich though still buying only one ticket at a time — could ever understand. For Lenny, luck was less connected to fantasy than it was to the very blood that ran through his veins.

I thought about my grandmother who was also pretty lucky but never quite saw it that way.

She too was a survivor, someone who got away, from Europe, from the Holocaust — while much of her family never did — and then got to live with her daughter and grandchildren in Flushing, Queens, with all the food she could cook, which she did like no one else in the world, along with two TVs and a credit card nestled safely somewhere in my father's wallet, and, of course, that chandelier with the five lights. Still, she would never consider herself lucky, no, just not unlucky — not yet anyway — for she believed if she looked luck in the face for even a second — it would all disappear, everything, so while the rest of us would curse our luck, always fantasizing about bigger and brighter things, my grandmother would sit alone in a corner, her hands ringing an ancient towel, making sure those five lights would never burn out.

Chapter 3

MY STORY, MY LOVER

This was my last reading. I didn't prepare. I drank a glass of wine. I always know not to drink alcohol before a reading — I read to about six people. Four of them were readers. One of them was a singer. She reminded me of Isabella Rossellini in Blue Velvet. I read like it was my last reading. Sometimes I came to a line that was like a tangled wire that I couldn't unravel no matter what I did. That seemed to make no sense. It was if my own lines betrayed me, twisted themselves into knots. When I read my story I felt great resistance. What seemed alive and funny in the past suddenly felt dry and lifeless. Among the six people at the bar one giggled once. This was my last reading. My story told me so. It resented me for not really wanting to read it. Let's be honest. I no longer had the desire to read it like I once did. And my story knew it.

Wouldn't a woman you no longer wanted to be with, to make love to her, know it too? Isn't my story like such a woman? My story hated me for my indifference. "Two can play at this game," it seemed to say to me. And the audience knew it. And the darkness knew it. That it was my last reading. "Good," I thought. "Let it be my last reading. What do I care? Let me finish this for the last time. Let me come to my last line ever and take my leave."

Then something happened. It was around the part when the narrator wonders whether all along his very existence has been ill-defined, wondering whether or not he has lived a life full of all the wrong definitions, a startling idea to contemplate — especially with a beautiful girl's hand on his thigh — that I suddenly started to enjoy, to really own the story again. I remembered the time we — my story and I — spent together — at times splitting apart, at times becoming a single entity as we tried to figure it all out. All that drama. The frustrations, the rejections, the accusations and counter-accusations, the false starts, the inevitable collapses, yet sticking together until the day — was it a rainy Sunday when I was listening to Bach or was it a dry Wednesday while I was listening to Zeppelin? I don't remember but I do remember how it all suddenly came together. For us. For both of us. Me and my story. And now I was back in my story, I loved it again. I thought how Matthew Arnold's true love in "Dover Beach" must have been — not a woman necessarily, or even another man — but his own poetry, "Ah, love, let us be true/To one another . . . for the world. . .Hath really neither joy, nor love, nor light . . . here as on a darkling plain . . . Where ignorant armies clash by night." "Ah, yes love," I thought, as I read my story now, "let us try to be true to each other for really who else do we have here tonight in this darkness and cold and the blaring sirens and the cell phones ringing and the mindless fingers texting and the inconsiderate and indifferent voices filtering in from the street like cigarette smoke? Us, that's who."

So I even forgot the audience. They didn't matter. But they too — as few as they were — started to listen. I could tell. I could feel them listening. I was glad because I also knew we needed them as much as we needed ourselves.

When I finished reading, my story and I were okay with each other again. I gently smoothed it out as if the paper it was written on was the smooth yet imperfect flesh of a lover and then gently slipped it back into my bag and after saying my goodbyes I too slipped away into the darkness. Was it my last reading? Perhaps. Perhaps not. Perhaps I will never come back. Then again maybe I will, for really when it comes down to it what choice do I — and my secret lover — now safely tucked away in the darkness of my black bag — really have?

Chapter 4

TO LIVE AND DIE IN FLUSHING

What is it about Flushing? Why is it that every time I go back to Flushing I think I'm going back for good this time, to live out the rest of my life and then die there?

The poet Stephen Stepanchev who is from Chicago but lived in Flushing for a very long time — including the time he was my poetry teacher at Queens College once called Flushing "The Center of the Universe" and certainly for almost 40 years it was mine.

Brooklyn is my home now but it is not my essence. It never entered my bloodstream — my soul if you will — for good or bad like Flushing did.

I know it is wrong to want to go home. Ask Thomas Wolfe.

But there is a pull for sure — but perhaps it is an unhealthy pull. I don't know. I do know I start to get excited whenever I plan a trip to Flushing but it's just as true that Flushing isn't quite the Flushing I remember.

Still it's there.

I still recognize it — still feel it — through its new facade, its new human and concrete identity, its Asian restaurants and groceries and beauty salons and mini malls.

It's not what's been replaced or added it's what still remains or, better yet, not so much what is still visible but what is invisible that pulls me back.

I think of Ishmael's words in Moby Dick.

"Though in many of its aspects this visible world seems formed in love, the invisible spheres were formed in fright."

I am no Ishmael.

I was never exiled. I never wandered.

I stayed put — in Flushing.

My wandering consisted perhaps of a journey of half a city block to a quiet corner of the playground where I would try to imagine myself as someone or someplace else — but I just couldn't.

I just could not imagine myself anywhere else but Flushing.

When I go back to Flushing — I can't quite escape the invisible — something is unresolved. There is someone I need to see. There is something I need to do.

Besides eat good Chinese food or go shopping in a Korean supermarket.

It's that young boy I look for in the playground — the playground that is still there despite the fact you need a key to get in now. Why?

Maybe to keep the old ghosts in or the new condos out.

The Flushing I knew is like a painting beneath a painting. Pentimento Flushing. Changed, altered.

But the Flushing in my soul alters not when alteration finds.

The street in front of my old apartment building may lead to a different place but still it is the first street I learned to cross—

The sky, the trees outside that second floor window is the same sky, the same trees that inspired my first words—

My first verse of poetry—

My first story—

The window from which my Grandmother's ghost still looks out in fear. Still stares beyond the visible.

At something the rest of us can neither see nor understand. Yet still fear.

We have been to lunch at a dumpling restaurant on Prince Street just off Main in downtown Flushing.

On the way back to his apartment, we pass the playground and I ask my brother to open the gate with his private key.

I always wanted one of those private keys.

I show my daughter where I used to play box ball or bench ball or where the old sandbox and sprinklers used to be.

I almost show her where my ghost sits — inside the small tunnel that leads back to the gate — but I decide to leave him alone.

I wanted to tell him that he turned out okay. That there was nothing to fear after all.

That he has a daughter now who will never be afraid to imagine something else or some place else.

That she will remember a Flushing without ghosts. One that was formed not in fright but in love.

But I think that young boy must know that by now.

Chapter 5

OLD MAN HUSTLE

Well I've done the old man hustle — that small bar on Essex Street just past Hester — where the ghosts of my ancestors hustled their wares to survive. I'm still hustling my stories trying to survive in a different way — so I don't despair too much. I thought about reading an old story bringing out some vintage tonight. It's a hot muggy night and I just don't feel like hustling anything on a night like this.

Standing on the subway platform in what must be around 120 degrees, I start dripping from head to foot until the train comes and then head towards the unforgiving ugliness, the raw beauty of the Lower East Side. Then the moment I climb up the subway stairs and stick my head into the street, it's like Mr. Spock staring into the face of Kollos the Medusan ambassador — Star Trek of course — sans visor, going mad — showing that even a Vulcan can go mad if he looks at something too hideous. But at the same time being a Vulcan and already having mind-melded with this rather brilliant and distinguished box of tangled light, Spock has seen the beauty inside the ugliness, the beauty inside the truth. "Is there no Truth in beauty?" That was actually the name of the episode taken from a line in a George Herbert poem. Facing the truth is tough.

If there was any way way to describe this still non-gentrified part of the Lower East Side, it is the Truth, the Real. If Hemingway saw NYC as a novel, he would have called this part of it that One True Sentence he always talked about. I remember when I was in college roaming the streets down here with my friends, drunk and depressed looking for a bar like in The Iceman Cometh and when I think I've found one with that stale beer smell and sawdust on the floor, I order a drink and then drop my head on the bar. Oh how I suddenly missed those days — the days of deep despair when I thought to be a real writer — especially in NY — where so many great writers were in despair, who drank themselves to death, who collapsed outside of bars and leaped off boats and were beaten up by sailors — you had to be in despair — or you couldn't be a real writer and what better place to feel despair, than in NYC and what better place in NYC than in the Lower East Side? It was there where I always felt the most like a struggling tormented writer. Ah Rivington, Bowery, Baxter, Division, Essex how you stirred my imagination.

Of course that's all it ever was — my imagination. After all, unlike Spock I could look into the face of Kolos without going mad knowing I always had my safety net, my nice middle class comfortable home in Queens to go back to, where I could dream of being the great writer living in despair, living on the edge of spiritual and physical and mental annihilation and then to sit on the edge, the very edge of my bed — eating a box of mallomars to console myself.

The Old Man Hustle bar isn't the kind of bar I remember hanging out in down here.

Though still wedged in along a row of stores on a pretty raw looking street, it isn't like that, it's more cool and sexy and young people drink beer and wine for hours and hours, who don't seem to get drunk at least not in any self-consciously dramatic way. I'm afraid Eugene O'Neil might have passed this one up. There's two small areas — other than the bar itself — one kind of a window seat the other where the reading takes place — well lit, a mic at the ready, really as inviting a place to read as any place I've been. Nayanda — creator of the Say What Production readings, hands me two red chips good for two free drinks. So this night I bring out my classic Queens story, "Cherry Orchard," my only story with a female narrator, good old Angie, who's pissed at her boyfriend for never listening to her and then for threatening to get rid of the cherry tree — the one she loves so much in his backyard — and replacing it with a swimming pool.

At first it's not easy being Angie and then she just takes me over completely — she's all those tough smart Queens Italian girls — Richmond Hill, Ozone Park, Howard Beach, Maspeth, the Rockaways — I knew in school, much smarter than the boyfriends and husbands they would end up with. When I finish reading, the first thing I've got to do is to shake

Tony's image, that big hollow chested hulking image out of my mind — and tell myself that I am really not having his baby, that this was all make believe and I am not really Angie.

That usually takes a few drinks. This time I order a shot of tequila — I think it was tequila — then another. People are still smiling at me. They must think I'm Angie. I have another shot. Just one more before going home. Any moment I expect my head to hit the bar. "Let him be," everyone will say. "He's a writer. He should be drunk. After all, he's probably in despair." They will take pictures. They will say to their friends, "That's the writer. First he was this Italian girl from Queens and then drank two shots and was out cold. And he was here. He was here with us."

But nothing happens. My head does not hit the bar. Yes, I am high, but more high from having been this exasperated Italian girl from Queens for the last 15 minutes, from having read to a group of people who seemed to really enjoy what I was reading — more than the two shots of tequila.

Worst of all, and to all you aspiring writers who worship the cult of despair — who believe you cannot really write about despair without being in despair yourself — I mean not really and perhaps in the long run you are right — and perhaps I too would have been a better writer if I had remained in despair — I would advise you to stop reading this now — because I have to say in all honesty that when I left Old Man Hustle I was happy — yes, so happy in fact that O'Neil himself would have sneered at me and shook his head in despair.

Chapter 6

THE SMELL OF CINNAMON BUNS

I'm at Remsen Graphics the copy place across the street from St. Francis College making a copy of my father's Army discharge papers.

"This is to certify that F.E. Levenberg staff sergeant 29th evacuation hospital is hereby Honorably Discharged from the military service of the USA. Separation Center Fort Dix, NJ 21 December 1945."

He was in the Army for 4 years and 22 days. He was overseas for 8 months and 3 days.

Under the heading "Battles and Campaigns," where someone typed in "None," my father penciled in "Luzon."

I remember my father's photos of the severed heads of Japanese soldiers brought back to his camp in Luzon by Philippine guerillas.

In a journal entry dated June 25, 1945 he says:

"Two Japs filtered into our area. The guerilla guards got them and cut off their heads. So there is peace in death. Heads looked young, rather clean cut looking."

When I first saw those photos I couldn't sleep at all, had the lights on all night and kept checking my parents' room to make sure their heads were still attached to their bodies.

When I asked my father how he felt about seeing those severed heads he just said, "What can I say? That's war."

When the graphics guy brings back my copy he says, "40 cents, please" and I can't believe it costs only 40 cents to copy a part of WWII.

When I tell him it's my father's discharge papers from WWII, he says "Oh yeah?" — in that kind of faux enthusiasm of a generation mired in indifference — so I can tell right away he's not really that interested, but the old man standing next to me says, "Oh yeah?" like I just woke something up in him, like he's the ancient mariner who no one listens to anymore.

"My brother was in the 34th Evacuation Unit," he says. "Oh yeah?" I say back and then suddenly the "Oh Yeahs" are flying back and forth — like missiles over the sea of Japan.

My father was in the 29th Evacuation Unit," I tell him.

"Oh yeah?" He says and then he tells me everything.

His name is Gene. He grew up around the Brooklyn Navy Yard and joined the Army when he was 15 and a half. He said he had no idea what he was getting into until he suddenly found himself in North Africa.

Later he served on the *U.S.S. Shea* which went to Okinawa to assist with minesweeping and anti-aircraft operations and then on to Iwo Jima and then he told me how months later a Yokosuka MXY-7 rocket powered Kamikaze plane (he said they called them Bakas — "fool" or "idiot" in Japanese) hit the ship so fast and so hard he hardly knew what happened — where it came from — where it went — and how — just like that — 40 men had been killed and over 80 wounded.

Later, while lining up to receive a Purple Heart with all the other survivors, he suddenly smelled cinnamon buns — it had been years since he smelled cinnamon buns — he thought the kitchen was destroyed and now he thought he might be smelling things — post traumatic shock.

But at that time what wasn't post or pre or just shock?

The whole time he was there in the Pacific — like in Okinawa or Iwo Jima — every ten steps someone else got blown up.

Go figure.

Shock meant nothing.

These guys were tough.

Nobody got shocked anymore.

No these were cinnamon buns he smelled all right. The kitchen had blown too.

But kitchen or no kitchen, he knew with a kind of certainty he hadn't felt in a long time — he could smell cinnamon buns and he was getting off this line — Purple Heart be damned.

And he was right.

And even though he never got his Purple Heart he did get his cinnamon buns and the whole time he's telling me this

I know he's still smelling them like he was still standing on that line almost 70 years ago.

When he told me this story I thought of course about my own father — the man who wrote about the food during the war as much as the battles that still raged in the Philippine mountains or the occupation of Japan — about the big chickens and the radishes — so big my father said because they used human feces to grow them.

He was in the 29th Evacuation Unit in the Philippine jungle. He was a medical laboratory technician who got excited whenever he got the chance to sew up bullet wounds or help treat lepers.

There is a photo of my father sitting on a beach chair in front of his tent holding a beer looking like he was sitting in the backyard of my aunt and uncle's house in Whitestone, Queens during a holiday BBQ.

After Gene finished his story he had that same smile my father had sitting in that beach chair like the world is crazy — always has been — always will be — and that if you can grab a chicken or a cinnamon bun even in the midst of human madness and chaos and world conflagration — go for it. For isn't it true? That while wars come and go, while people live and die, the smell of a cinnamon bun lasts forever?

Chapter 7

UNPERCHED

I cannot pass my neighbor down the block without her wanting to introduce a neighbor of hers, a young writer working on a novel, who just moved in next door to her. I think I made the mistake once of telling her I'd like to meet him, so ever since she cannot see me without telling me whether he's home or not and if he is home whether or not I'd like her to ring his bell and introduce us.

I'm usually not in the mood or else I'm on my way somewhere else which I usually am if I'm passing her house, or anxious to get home from having been somewhere else, like work, so I tell her next time.

This evening, the evening of my reading at The Perch Café around the corner, is no exception.

"I just saw him" she tells me.

"Oh, yeah?" I say. "Just now?"

"Yeah," she says. "He just left his house not 10 minutes ago."

"What a shame," I say. "Maybe I can catch him later."

"That's too bad," she says. "I mean he was just here."

I cannot describe the disappointment in her voice and in her face, as if this meeting, this meeting not particularly, or at least not enthusiastically sought after by either me or the young writer, was the most important meeting since Reagan and Gorbachev, Napoleon and Goethe, Pound and Eliot, or perhaps even Stanley and Livingston.

I'm on my way to The Perch Café to do a reading, my second one there since last May. I'm supposed to meet my friend Marilynn for dinner and whoever else shows up.

When I get there, about 6:05 p.m., Marilynn is not there yet. I start to look at the menu and realize I don't have my glasses. I cannot read my stories without my glasses so I go back home to get them.

On the way home she stops me again and says, "You wouldn't believe it. He just came back.

Not two minutes after you left. If you want I can ring his bell . . ."

But I tell her how I'm in a hurry now, how I have to get my glasses and then get right back to The Perch where I'm doing a reading. I tell her to let him know and maybe he can meet me there. Then she gives me his card.

This pleases her as if we are getting closer to meeting, although in reality nothing has changed. He will neither come to my reading nor will I call the number on the card. When I pass by her house once again, after retrieving my glasses, she doesn't say anything but just smiles, a satisfactory smile as if she has done all she can, at least for today, to bring us together although in reality . . .

When I get back to The Perch, Marilynn is still not there. I order an iced coffee although what I really want is a glass of wine, but I know that any alcohol in my system won't do me much good, will flatten out my voice as well as the stories.

At about 6:20, Marilynn shows up. She got lost. Before we even order any food, others start arriving. There's Francois Snapping Turtle and his wife who go back to the garden to sit.

Later, shortly before I read, I will glimpse Francois and his wife sipping white wine at a small table near the door looking like Maurice Chavalier and Hermoine Gingold singing "Yes, I remember it well," from Gigi.

In a few more minutes, Florence arrives, my 90 year old student who has never shown up to class without her daughter. She asks me if someone might give her a ride back to the subway later only because the walk back is uphill.

In a few more minutes Jason Dubow, an English professor from St. Francis College, arrives with his entire family, including his two sons, 9 and 11. This is the first time I start to think about the "adult content" in the short stories I'll be reading tonight, "Cherry Orchard" and "The Homeless." Don't Jason and his wife care? And if not, whatever that reason might be shouldn't I feel the same way and not have sent my daughter home earlier with my wife?

Should I have explained to her how it's my characters doing and saying things and not me?

Still, I know she knows I'm the one writing those words, creating those situations, and finally, reading it all out loud to strangers.

To my daughter my fantasies are my reality; I am my imagination; my imagination is me.

No, when Angela screams at Tony in "The Cherry Orchard," "Fuck you Tony," it's me screaming "Fuck you Tony," and when Tony shouts back "Fuck you Angela" it's me shouting back "Fuck you Angela" and when Tony digs his fingernails into Angela's ass, it's me digging my fingernails into Angela's ass.

For her I am the inventor, the creator, the god who made these characters out of the flesh of my own imagination. It's not them. It's me. They don't exist, but I do, and if I am not Everyman, at the very least I am every one of my own characters.

It's like when the Victoria's Secret commercial comes on TV, she always tells me not to look at it because even if I'm not thinking what she thinks I'm thinking, to her I'm thinking it anyway, and what could she possibly think I'm thinking?

This is what scares me. This is why I send her home. And when I finish reading the two stories, I look up and there's Jason's two young boys, looking exactly the way they looked when they first walked in, a bit indifferent, somewhat bored, and most likely wishing they too had already been sent home.

Chapter 8

COFFEE

Does it bother me that coffee beans could be extinct by 2080?

Not really since by that time I'd be off the stuff permanently, I assume. On the other hand, just the juxtaposition of the words coffee and extinct sends chills down my spine and lethargy spreading throughout my nervous system. So just to shake those feelings I've been drinking more coffee than ever. Usually I make more coffee in the morning than I drink. If I drink one cup and my wife drinks one there's about two more left in the pot. Rather than leaving it in there to get cold and eventually spilled out, I bought a stainless steel state of the art thermos — a thermos that will keep my coffee warm till hell freezes over — and bring that coffee to work. With such a gloom and doom forecast about the future of coffee beans why waste a single drop ever again?

Those two extra cups of coffee every morning provide me with the absolute certainty that I can accomplish anything — with that sudden terrifying feeling of elation I savor like that last drop of hot coffee in a heatless mug — provide me with the desire to love the world and figure out how to save it all in one streaming heart-pounding thought — all before 11 a.m. when the feeling starts to fade away and I am once again a shriveling anxious emotional wreck lacking all confidence, quickly losing the will to live.

I often think of the Star Trek episode — "Spock's Brain" when Dr. McCoy dons the helmet of knowledge — known as "The Great Teacher" — to reattach Mr. Spock's brain which had been stolen by a group of dumb extraterrestrial blondes — the Eymorgs — to help save their civilization. Dr. McCoy's immense medical knowledge, though extremely helpful, is still not enough to reattach Spock's brain. But the moment he dons "The Great Teacher," everything suddenly becomes very clear — much like for me when I quaff my first cup of coffee in the morning. "Of course, of course. A child could do it. A child could do it," Dr. McCoy exclaims. But just like my first cup of coffee in the morning — or my espresso in the afternoon — this feeling can't last forever. "I am trying to thread a needle with a sledgehammer," Dr. McCoy exclaims once the helmet begins to lose its power and alas Spock himself has to talk him through the rest of the rather mind-boggling experience.

And so it is with me and my coffee and — better yet — my first cup of espresso in the afternoon. I am all powerful. "Of course" I exclaim to myself — suddenly figuring out the meaning of the universe — or more importantly a good ending to a story or essay I have been agonizing over for days — "A child could have figured that out," I cry out to no one in particular. But then, just like that, it all starts to fade away and suddenly I am myself again, edgy, anxious, uncertain. "Was it all just an illusion?" I think to myself. Is it really so healthy for me — physically and mentally — to daily experience the ecstasy of heaven and the horrors of hell and all before noon? No, I have to end this — I have to leave that thermos of extra coffee home every day — force myself to go out into the cold, across the street and buy a cup. And the espresso? Well, maybe every other day and then maybe twice a week and then . . .once? But gradually, slowly. . . there's no rush — not today anyway — for now I might just need one small cup to figure out a good ending to this.

Chapter 9

COLD BROOKLYN

It's been cold in Brooklyn lately. My office for example. Just last week it was warm enough to be a sauna. This week it was as cold as a meat locker. I usually complain to facilities management if it's too hot but almost never if it's too cold because then it will go right back to being hot again.

What did Frost say?

Some say the world
Will end in fire
Some say in ice
From what I've tasted
Of desire
I hold with those who favor
fire
But if it had to perish twice
I think I know enough of
hate
To say that for destruction
Ice is great
And would suffice.

Did Frost ever sit in my office?

I always loved that poem. Maybe I like what it says or the clever rhymes which seem to fit into snug little corners. I don't know or care only that I really like it and it is one of the few poems I've committed to memory — probably because it's short enough to memorize. If you want to know the truth. But that's why one reads poetry for the truth and quickly. In "Streetcar Named Desire," a play I happen to love, Blanche is a mad elitist otherworldly poet who says things like "Suddenly there's God" and "I shall die of eating an unwashed grape," and of course "I have always depended on the kindness of strangers." There's fire and desire in this play but where's the ice?

It's in the unmeltable fear that drives poets mad and sends them off to asylums — that's where.

But still Williams always seems to make bad physical surroundings and difficult human situations pretty lush and sexy and wonderfully tragic and filled with beautiful sentences.

Getting back to my office (must I?) it's hard to say which I'd rather work in — the heat of desire, or the cold unforgiving winds of hate. I try working on a new story. I think of calling it "Brooklyn Chaud."

I think if I write in a really warm room it will come out lush and sexy. I take the thinnest paperback I have and use it as a fan. The real fan in the room, the little electric one they gave all of us during a particularly hot month, keeps flying off the table. Yet all I end up writing is a sweaty story about people who sweat too much. There's not much action. People are too lethargic to move or say what's on their minds. I have to speak for them. They cannot speak for themselves. The story is static. The fan has flown off the table for the last time. I email facilities management and tell them I am in danger of passing out.

I think of poker night in Streetcar. I call it Streetcar — even in my mind — because I can barely say the word Desire. I think of Gregor Samsa waking up on a cold morning in Prague and suffering — entymologically of course — from a myriad of stiff joints. In this way I try to cool off. I think of *Call of the Wild*, *White Fang*, *Ethan From*, *Little Women*, *Dr. Zhivago*, *Winter Dreams*, Gerald Crich, dying in the snow in *Women In Love*. Nothing works. But I realize reading the books are more effective perhaps than recalling them.

One morning I open the door to my office and I am welcomed by icy winds blowing through that dreaded vent in the ceiling. I place my coffee on my desk piping hot and by the time I remove my coat and sit down it has turned to ice coffee. If I wanted ice coffee, I would have ordered ice coffee I say to myself.

I imagine cutting a hole in the floor and going ice fishing. I'm turning blue. Perhaps if I think of those hot sultry nights in the New Orleans of "Streetcar Named Desire" — and now by the way I can say Desire — or Fahrenheit 451, Towering Inferno, the Long Hot Summer, To Kill a Mockingbird, Inherit the Wind — the jury, the spectators, waving those small hand fans trying to cajole, to convince, whatever air there is in the room to change its molecular structure if just for a few hours. When things get really bad I imagine myself nude wrestling with Gerald Crich in the Alps which are melting beneath our feet and other exposed parts of us because of global warming.

I try to write a story about Brooklyn in the cold. I think of calling it "Brooklyn Froid." But that story moves too quickly as if it keeps trying to keep warm. It took too many short cuts, cut too many corners, and no matter how I tried to get it to a boiling point it wouldn't boil, but stayed stiff as a stalactite. My words wore a heavy coat. They did not breathe normally. They huddled together. They were definitely not themselves.

I had never realized how important the temperature in a room was for me to write well.

When I first started writing I always imagined those great tubercular writers starving in some Parisian garret — freezing in the winter and roasting in the summer and still producing great literary classics. How will I ever be a great writer if I'm so picky? But don't you think those garret writers would rather have written in a nice comfortable den, well heated in the winter, well cooled in the summer somewhere in the Berkshires? And what about the German Nobel winner Heinrich Boll who didn't want to switch to an electric typewriter because of the humming sound?

As for me, I'll be honest with you. Put me in a bubble. A Writer's bubble. Not too hot. Not too cold. Plenty of coffee. An endless supply of cold cuts. A clean dimly lit bathroom. Then give me that Condors quill, Vesuvius' crater for an inkstand (Melville) and I am ready to break the frozen sea within you (Kafka) and make you so cold no fire can warm your body (Dickinson).

That is as long as it stays no more than 72 degrees in here.

Chapter 10

READING WITHOUT GLASSES

The prompt for my senior citizen class today was "a crushed pizza box causes a sensation at the museum." Our first reader forgot her glasses. She wrote about a character finding a crushed pizza box which later is hailed by the museum director as a masterpiece of abstract art. As she read I did notice a disconnect kind of thing going on but imagined it was for effect — a kind of intentional disunity of language and meaning, almost as if she were skipping lines. Later Ellen told me she was skipping lines, not to create any particular effect — she had no such intention — but because she had trouble seeing. Wasn't Monet and other Impressionists thought to be near- sighted? And wasn't this responsible for one of the great art movements in history?

This reminded me of the time I did a reading at a bar in Williamsburg, Brooklyn back in the early 90's when I first discovered I needed reading glasses. I remember being on a stage where the lighting wasn't very good and when I looked at my story, I suddenly realized I could barely make out the words. So I began to read slowly, deliberately, word by word, as if I were intentionally trying to create a world in slow motion like in a film when the camera tries to slow down a bullet fired from a gun or an intentional distortion of human mouths in the midst of verbal confrontation. Indeed the story was a story about the attempt to slow things down, to examine human behavior and action in a measured and deliberate way. But it was really the fact that I could not see very well, that I could barely make out the words, that suddenly without warning like a cruel joke like something out of one of my own stories I had become far-sighted. At certain times the stress and strain of making out my own words, of combining them with others to form sentences — of the very struggle of getting to the finish line — was almost too much to bear, and yet when I finally finished reading, I felt I had been up there for hours, and much to my surprise, the audience actually applauded, enthusiastically even, and when I returned to my table, all my friends congratulated me for the interesting way I read the story. You gave it the ominous post-apocalyptic tone it needed, one friend said. Needless to say we are no longer friends. That's the kind of comment you say to yourself and not aloud. It was as if having almost drowned in rough waters my flailing and thrashing had been seen by others as a new type of breast stroke. "Well done," they'd call out. "You really looked like you were drowning."

I was.

I began to wonder. Is a story a story because of the way I see it? Does it cease to exist the moment I close my eyes or my vision becomes too blurred to read it without glasses? No. The story is done. It has a life of its own, its own voice that I — its creator — has given it. It must not and can not become a victim or slave of the reader's bad vision or physical and mental condition at the time. There are all sorts of physical conditions under which you can read a story. I've read a story after a few beers and found myself reading without much of an edge or any real emotion but more of a high pitched over-emotion.

And then what about reading with a headache when only relentless pain seems to accompany the characters' world or when you're in a bad mood, or good mood, or existential mood or post structural mood? You can't be sure of anything. It's too unpredictable.

The next time I read that story — and right before I uttered a single word — I decided to take my glasses off. But when I did it was all a blur. My eyes had gotten even worse than the last time. I could barely make out a single word. This time I thought I would truly drown. So I put my glasses back on because I knew the very least I owed my story was to see where it would lead me.

Chapter 11

REMEMBERING LINCOLN

In November of 1963, a woman turned to my father on line at the bank and said — referring to President Kennedy's recent assassination — "I don't know if I'll ever get over this," and my father said, "I still haven't gotten over Lincoln."

Me too. Since the day I was born, I haven't gotten over Lincoln. I think the moment we Lincoln-philes are born, we cry for Lincoln. If you think we stare at some circus mobile over our cribs, you're wrong — we are in our still inchoate mind's eye watching John Wilkes Booth crashing onto the stage of Ford's theater exclaiming Sic Semper Tyrannus — ever thus to tyrants — the state motto of Virginia. That's the first Latin sentence I ever learned.

When I visited Ford's theater — where Lincoln was shot — and the Peterson house — where he died — I was 10 years old and felt somehow I had been there before. I seem to remember seeing the blood stained pillow he died on. Probably not — someone must have cleaned the bed clothes after that — some maid no doubt must have made the bed. But the idea of blood stains made him more human — the idea that Lincoln — like any tragic figure in history or literature could reach such heights and then just bleed into a stranger's pillow and die like anyone else was at the very least — disheartening.

Speaking of blood, somehow Abraham Lincoln has always flowed in mine — I mean what did I know of basic human rights, of slavery, of preserving the union when I was 10? Yes, I was no doubt affected by his mythical, god-like status, in the history books when I was growing up. The rail splitter, Honest Abe, lying on the cold floor of his log cabin in the backwoods of Kentucky reading by the fire — walking 10 miles in the snow to return library books — wrestling Jack Armstrong and falling in love with Ann Rutledge, whom of course I had a crush on even though I had no idea what she looked like. In a world where everyone seemed flawed and wrong all the time — my world that is — I always believed

Abe Lincoln was always right and that he was as good as good could be. "Let us judge not that we be not judged," he says — quoting the Bible — in his second inaugural address — and as a young boy who felt judged all the time, I always believed he meant me as much as anyone else.

He was tall and gangly and apparently, for his time, very ugly — almost ape-like to his enemies. Edwin Stanton, his second and last Secretary of War, and the man who uttered those immortal words the moment he died, "Now he belongs to the ages" was originally, as Doris Kearns Goodwin would call him, a "rival" of Lincoln's in a famous law case. According to Stanton, Lincoln was the "original gorilla," and that "Du Chaillu" (famous African explorer who apparently confirmed the existence of gorillas for Americans) was a fool to wander all the way to Africa in search of what he could so easily have found in Springfield, Il.." Little did Stanton know — though somewhere inside him he probably did — that this apparent "ape," this gangly, physically deformed and slightly blemished man (there was that large mole above the right side of his lips) who never even knew how to comb his hair — would end up having that face carved on a mountain one day.

It's true in most of his photos Lincoln looks like a physical exaggeration of what a human should look like — his arms, his legs, his ears — he was our first bearded president and I don't mean mutton chops like John Quincy Adams or Martin Van Buren — he was a throwback to the sage, the philosopher, the prophet — "Father Abraham," they called him and not just the slaves.

"I see very plainly Abraham Lincoln's dark brown face," Walt Whitman says in Specimen Days, "with the deep-cut lines, the eyes always to meet me with a deep latent sadness in the expression . . . None of the artists or pictures has caught the deep, though subtle and indirect expression of the man's face. There is something else there. One of the great portrait painters of two or three centuries ago is needed."

That could possibly explain why I often spend hours staring at Lincoln's photos — always searching for that "something else" in his face — trying to understand why I felt and still feel about him, something that goes beyond simple fascination. Indeed, I may never know and perhaps I never want to know. What joy there always is for me just contemplating Lincoln's face and never understanding it.

Even with all the post-modern historical revisionism associated with Lincoln's racism or despotism (you mean Booth was right?) after all, he wanted to colonize the freed slaves and would not want his sister (if he had a sister) to marry one. He also suspended habeas corpus and played around with a constitution he sent thousands to their deaths to preserve. He was a man of contradictions — no question — but it was his contradictions that formed the complex, bigger than life, tragic figure — that made him flawed and which made him human. And as a human being and not a god or statue or carving on a mountain he showed how a person can grow, can change uncertainty and indecision into true greatness.

I couldn't wait to see the movie with Daniel Day-Lewis. When I first saw the billboard overlooking the West Side Highway in Manhattan, I fell in love all over again. Those eyes, that mouth, those lips, that dark heavy brow — like a precipitous cliff — like dark foreboding clouds before a storm — always that inscrutable look of pain and sadness — not just for his own life but for everyone's life — because his own life, his own heart and soul, belonged to everyone from the moment he was born until the moment he died.

This is the brooding — that quintessential brooding (and who is better at brooding than Daniel Day Lewis?) that not only saved democracy but brought back its dignity.

I was not disappointed. It was as if Lincoln himself, the human Lincoln, concerned husband and father, getting on the floor with his beloved son Willie, arguing with his wife Mary, slapping his oldest son Robert; wily politician in his efforts — behind the scenes — to pass the Thirteenth Amendment; that wonderful backwoods, high-pitched voice that always seemed to ring, to resonate above the fray — was on that screen for two hours.

It was only that very last scene that somewhat bothered me. Could it just have ended with him going off to the theatre? I mean who doesn't know the rest? Did they have to show him lying there bleeding again in that bedroom across the street with Edwin Stanton saying — still again — how "he belonged to the ages."? Did I really need that? Did the film have to remind me how much I have still not gotten over it?

Chapter 12

WHY I WRITE

Christina Vines a wonderful fiction writer — we read together at Franklin Park last January — and moderator of a reading series at 2A — a restaurant and bar at 2nd Street and Avenue A — asked me to write a short piece on "why I write."

The following is what I came up with a couple of days ago while walking my dogs in Prospect Park. I tried to be as honest as I could — to myself as well as to all the writers and readers out there — without sounding too pretentious or dishonest — because necessarily, and for the most part, the writing process is more unconscious than conscious and so are the reasons for writing and that once you start explaining or analyzing it you may actually be moving further away, not closer, to the answer.

Anyway, here goes:

I don't have to write. But if I didn't I wouldn't be very happy.

Writing helps me make sense of the world and everything about the world that's in my head. Writing helps me learn things about myself and other people I didn't know. Writing makes me calm.

I feel very satisfied when I write and especially when I finish something I'm writing as if I just filled a deep hole, or closed a deep wound, or just paved a road inside me that was starting to buckle.

Writing helps me live peacefully with my thoughts and with my neighbors' thoughts.

When a succubus sits on my chest at night, writing something very wry and very ironic usually gets rid of it or any other demons that happen to be lingering around.

Writing gives me the time and space I can't get doing anything else.

I could be sitting in the middle of Grand Central Station and feel protected and isolated by my writing. At the same time I could be standing with other people on line at the bank or on a train platform and feel overwhelmed.

Writing keeps me sane.

I don't really know why but if I didn't write I'd probably be in a padded room — heavily medicated.

Why do I write? Who knows? I try not to think about it too much.

Chapter 13

THE POWER OF CUBAN COFFEE

I see my mother everywhere. The food court is full of my mother not in a bad way but in a full way. She is waiting on line to buy us knishes. She is talking to a man who looks like my father with her chin raised just a little so she can look younger. She is 90 but she knows she can pass for 75. She has at least a quarter of a century fewer wrinkles than someone else her own age.

Now she sits outside the luggage discount store at the flea market dreaming of moving out of her house. A man sits at the same bench his stomach out, his legs spread. He snores. I am thinking he too snores who only sits and waits. When I return from my walk around the market stalls, my mother tells me to sit down. I tell her I don't want to sit down. She tells me I'm tired and I should sit. I think she's the one who's tired and wants to keep sitting, so I squeeze in between her and the snoring guy. I look over at the piano that plays itself. I think about how bad the economy is down here that they can't afford to hire a piano player and have to teach pianos to play themselves. Why would anyone want go listen to a piano playing itself ? Would anyone want to see an orchestra playing without musicians? A pair of shoes dancing without a dancer? A pair of polyester pants and a white belt without a man snoring in them?

I'm not certain why the men's room at the food court has the loudest most powerful hand blower I have ever seen or heard. Is it really necessary? Perhaps it would be more appropriate at the airport since it sounds a lot like a plane right before take off. I am thinking it was designed by a canasta group of elderly Jewish women who are sick and tired of their husbands leaving the men's room with wet hands.

It just reminds me of the lack of subtlety anywhere around here. I think of this food court not so much as a place to eat but as a place to put enormous amounts of food inside of me and wait for the results later.

There is one stand in particular that specializes in knishes. Although knishes, as far back as I can remember, were always sidekicks now they seem to be the main characters. They have shoved everything they can into them here. Even hot dogs. There are hot dogs now sticking out of knishes. Hot dog has now become an adjective phrase to describe a particular kind of knish. Can there possibly be a department anywhere in the world with the word health in it that should have let this happen? I really try to hide my daughter's eyes when we get to the display case. No matter how you slice it, it is not a wholesome sight. All that being said, however, whoever thought of it in the first place is a sick evil genius.

Right next to the "knish place" is "The First Avenue Deli" since the name "Second Avenue Deli" is already taken. I suppose they figured what's one avenue. You can't fool people though. Almost no one is buying anything there. Except me. I buy a hot dog. It's not until I get my Cuban coffee — when the meaning of the universe opens up to me — that I suddenly realize that there is no deli on Second ave. But that's okay. I am in a strangely forgiving mood. It is the power of Cuban coffee. It begins slowly and then suddenly I want to forgive the world for all its transgressions. I look around and notice people are happy. Even the old people are happy. They eat things like knishes and pizza like they're kids again. They laugh with their grandchildren. Sellers from different stalls are talking to each other. The world has become one big flea market. I could shop all day, buy things like little hats and tool kits and gold sequined iphone cases and bundled socks and reading glasses and all those gadgets they sell at three in the morning on TV which make so much more sense to me now. And I even feel sorry for the poor guy who sells that liquid soap that cleans glasses — where I have never seen anyone stop — and I almost buy a bottle except they haven't invented coffee — Cuban or otherwise — that powerful yet.

I hear that piano that plays itself again and look at it and listen to it with wonder, imagining a world one day when we will not have to lift a finger ever again when everything will be done for us and we won't even need piano players to play pianos or saxophonists to play the sax and we can shop, shop,

shop for things big and small and large and shove things into our mouths, foods we have known shoved inside foods we have never known and listen to music we have never heard and hear books read aloud from somewhere in the sky, while we are awake or dreaming, and as we leave the food court I see the man in the polyester pants still snoring on the bench and I envy him for I see he already has reached his own blessed ignorant happiness — to sleep guiltlessly while making bodily noises among an indifferent public while his wife shops — much to his unconscious pleasure — alone.

Later that evening, back at my mother's house, stomach acid begins to move slowly yet sinuously into my throat. My mother bemoans her fate, her age, her loneliness here in this apartment — alone now — my father, her friends and family, all gone. She can't find a bottle of pills she bought that morning at the pharmacy. "My eyes are no good anymore," she says.

That night, unable to sleep, I notice it too. At first I'm not sure what it is. And then I know. It is the silence. It is a silence I have never heard before. No wind in the trees, no voices across the lake, no cicadas or crickets hiding in the dark — even the phone doesn't ring — nothing. Now there is only the memory of sound — of years ago or even this afternoon — of pianos playing of fat men snoring — of hand dryers blowing — of the elderly eating knishes and pizza with their grandchildren — for, alas, the power of the Cuban coffee has vanished.

Chapter 14

REDEMPTION

It was a sultry kind of evening. I was doing a reading at The Linger Café on Atlantic Avenue in Brooklyn.

I walked over there from work — maybe a 20 minute or so walk, but lugging 10 copies of my book and wearing a sports jacket and long sleeved shirt in that lingering humidity, I was soaked through by the time I got there.

There was no air conditioning.

I ordered some food and what I thought might be a cold beer and found a table in the back garden. The beer was warm, the food too spicy, but I was joined by one of the readers and my former writing student, Dahlia Heyman and her friend Christine and we talked about writing and teaching writing for a while until a couple of my senior citizen students showed up.

There was Francois Snapping Turtle and his wife and Ellen Press-Scott and Lynette Fronenberger and Ingrid Celms and Rose Fontanella who came by Access-a-Ride and after a few minutes Lynette's allergy started to bother her so Ellen walked her home and neither would be coming back for the reading.

The Reading started about 8pm and Kat Chua, another former student of mine, who arranged the whole event she called Unboxed Voices, read a short piece about a young boy and his Opossum which I found quite delightful, which I happen to find most of her writing and in fact, she herself, to be.

Then it was my turn. I mentioned how I walked into a coffee shop one time because I was early for a date and there was a really old cruller sitting under a plastic case that I really wondered a lot about and when I do that I usually end up writing a story, so I figured what better story to start with than The Cruller, a story about a man much too early for a date who gets caught up in the microcosmic relationship between a waitress (whom he fantasizes much too much about, especially since he's about to go on a date) and the cigar-chomping owner of the coffee shop, both of whom are quite content to live in their own little coffee shop universe that has bad food and in particular a stale Cruller which the narrator is convinced will never be sold and it is of course that certainty that keeps their world warm, secure, and most of all happy and God help the customer who would in any way upset the perfect balance of that universe.

So I read the Cruller and a story that was always good for a few laughs got none, not even a titter and I think everything, the story, the characters came out real flat — the heat? The beer? The competing sounds of buses, trucks and ambulances, indifference? Maybe I figured the story would read itself and didn't really need me to do much except use my voice to move it along.

When I finished, in about 11 minutes, Kat announced I'd be back later and that my book was on sale and I couldn't help think that no one cared. Then Dahlia read, something she had actually started in my writing class at N.Y.U., and it was good and she read it well. Tammy followed with a narrative full of authentic red neck dialogue and a plot though not convoluted exactly, but convoluted enough and a bit too long, so that I felt, and I have a feeling the audience did too, because I was beginning to understand this audience in an intuitive sort of way, that it might have been easier to read along or read it ourselves or at least have a lot of cold, free beer in front of us while hearing about a guy who really liked beer.

And the whole time this is going on, that is between the time of me and me again, not that I wasn't listening to everyone else, but I was sitting real straight in my seat with my hands folded, almost in some sort of contrition for my earlier mistakes, contrition only for myself, no one else, and thinking, and feeling quite relieved really that I still had one more chance to redeem myself, and that I needed to read well, to know I had not walked to this place in the lingering humidity, lugging ten books, having invited all my friends, students and colleagues and then blown it.

It was kind of like Top Chef that begins with a quick fire competition, like a meal you have to cook in about 30 minutes as opposed to several hours and how often the best come out last or at least on the bottom third and I was feeling like that now.

When Kat called me back I just relaxed for a moment, took a deep breath before reading a story about a young woman who has trouble breathing, and ironically I was having a little trouble breathing normally at this time myself, which could only help in reading the part of poor Dyspnea.

The first thing I said was "Thanks for having me back," which got a laugh so immediately I knew at least I had their attention and that they were going to listen, they were going to give me a chance at redemption.

And from the very first line, "From the first day I knew her, she had trouble breathing.

"I . . .like . . .you . . .a lot," she said once and then was completely out of breath."

I knew I'd be okay; I knew I was inside my story, inside my character's heads. I was Dyspnea, tormented by her family, by her own conscience; I was the narrator who loved Dyspnea but felt desperate, frustrated, even guilty that he could not figure out a way to help her. From the moment when Dyspnea comes into her brother Ted's bedroom until the narrator takes her home again for her to "practice her screaming," I even began to choke up, actually had to hold back my tears to finish the story.

To me, and I believe to the audience as well, I had captured the very essence of my story, for whatever that's worth, and spoke that essence as honestly as I possibly could and with great love for my own characters.

And that is all I can ever hope for, can ever hope I can achieve as a writer and as a reader and with this story, with Dyspnea, I believe I did and when you can do that your audience knows it, feels it, and based on some wonderful and generous comments from audience members afterwards, I believe they did.

I even sold two books and got to speak to some interesting people and bid farewell to my friends and students, young and old, former and present, and no longer feeling quite as hot, or quite as burdened as before, my friend Donna drove me home, and I got back just in time to catch Top Chef.

Chapter 15

HOW CC SABATHIA BROKE
MY WRITING SLUMP

I'm not the first to think it, but I always thought that baseball and life were kind of similar — one kind of a metaphor or microcosm for the other — which one I'm not really sure but since life was supposedly created before baseball, though some, including myself, might disagree, I mean can't you picture big white bearded God a hell of a pitcher up there mowing down all the teams that hell could muster, way before even a single celled creature appeared on earth? Well I can. It makes as much sense as most other things we've been asked to picture or believe in all our lives. Regardless, let's call baseball a metaphor or microcosm for life.

A couple of weeks ago, the Orioles played the Yankees in a playoff game the winner of which would then have to win two more to get to the next playoff series and then win four in that series to get to the World Series, where they'd have to win four more to become champions of the world, the universe, maybe even heaven (neither team, however made it) and then only a few years down the line, their glory, unlike God's, begins to fade. Yes they are remembered — some people have to be reminded or to look them up on the internet forget — to remember they were once champions, the key words here 'remember' and 'once' and needless to say no matter how many replays we watch or stories we read about them it — that moment in time — at least for me, will never be the same again.

I have great memories of the 1969 Mets — I watched them on TV, went to games at Shea Stadium, even the last playoff game against the Atlanta Braves when I cut school and sat behind home plate and saw Hank Aaron hit a home run and 21 year old Nolan Ryan strike out Rico Carty with the bases loaded and went crazy when the game ended and the heretofore hapless Mets were going to the World Series and though the field filled up with thousands of fans ripping the field apart, all the guards — left with nothing to do — seemed determined not to let me so I couldn't get on the field but still I got to see, only moments later, as if by fate, the red headed girl from Flushing High School on whom I had a big crush, who smiled at me like she recognized me — as if I could have actually said hello to her all those years in the hallway and who after that day, that magical day, I still didn't say hello to because on that day, and that day only, not even the next day — anything was possible.

Anyway, back to that Yankees vs. Orioles playoff game. There was C.C. Sabathia — larger than life looking weary and pained, Hercules or Odysseus sweating profusely, pounding and pounding the strike zone never letting up like Hemingway's old man pounding one shark after another on the skull — he never seemed satisfied — each inning was his own Odyssey — one wrong pitch, one misplaced grounder, one bad call by the imperfect umpires and the team was doomed. Nothing else must enter his mind, not an iota of doubt or uncertainty about the outcome of this game, not the shouting of the enemy crowd imploring each batter to destroy him, to crush his every pitch, screaming "No, you won't do it . You can't do it. You will make that one fatal mistake which will unravel it all which will render your whole struggle meaningless and destined to be forgotten."

But he would not listen. Everything rested on this giant's shoulders — each out just meant there was another out to get — it was 2 - 2 in the 8th inning — 8 innings already seemed like a lifetime and his own warriors that stood loyally behind him, yet as feckless as their opponents — unable to score, to deliver the final blow but on perhaps, on the contrary bracing for their opponents final blow — fearing that their own leader might fall before his opponent did, knowing that he, Sabathia, had already made all the mistakes he would be allowed to make — this was a great struggle but still there was that human factor, the pitch count, after all, though looking more like a god tonight, still in reality, he was only human. Wasn't he?

And even though he was a Yankee (I hated the Yankees) still, suddenly, I loved him — Sabathia became my inspiration.

If necessary, I thought, he must go on forever. Keep pitching; 100 pitches, 200 pitches, 300 pitches until his arm came off. Then lift it high above his head to the jeering crowd, towards his enemy until they too, like his own warriors, would begin to cheer, could not help but cheer, that no matter what their minds told them, their heart knew differently.

When the Yankees broke through with five runs in the 9th inning it was truly anti-climactic. Deus ex machina? The gods apparently grew tired early and blew breath into the Yankees bats. Sabathia could rest now on his laurels — the gods and the Yankees said it was okay — have a beer, sneak in a subway, relax. The Orioles who struggled the whole game to score two runs were not about to score five more in one inning. But Sabathia was not satisfied. He was not about to let someone else finish his masterpiece, his great epic, his tragedy. He would complete what he started. He understood baseball and how much like life it was. That one finishes what one started — because if you let someone else finish the job no matter how easy it may seem, well you never know mostly because in baseball as in life "it ain't over till it's over." So there he was again coming out for the 9th inning, and there he was, as if the game were still tied, with that same serious focused pained look on his face, wanting that last out so badly and when he finally got it — a pop up to the infield which he pointed to as if he were pointing to the heavens — I watched him go into the dugout, the warrior returning home, and at last I saw the slightest smile break out.

But of course this game would blend into so many others. For example, his very next start he was in command from the very start; he never seemed to be struggling at all and shut out the Orioles 3 - 0. That one seemed too easy. It was the previous game I will remember for a long time — the one that made me remember the joy of being a writer, not when a story came easily, but the stories I had to struggle with, the ones I worked on day and night, the ones that mocked me, that would not cooperate, that taunted me, that tricked me into thinking I had it, that the end was right around the corner only to find another detour or dead end, a story that refused to unravel itself but on the contrary tighten itself like a stubborn fist — having to ignore my personal demons imploring me to quit, work on something else or the voices that echoed over and over in my head, "It's over it's over it's over. You will never do this. Maybe, just maybe you will never write again." And I realized that recently I have been listening too much to those demons, to the voices in my head and that watching Sabathia on the mound that night, I forgot I hated the Yankees, because I could only see another artist, an artist I wished I could be again. I saw the struggle I loved, the struggle I have missed, and the struggle I knew now I would have again.

Chapter 16

READING ELLIPSIS

My reading at Fiction Addiction the other night (sponsored by 2A on Ave. A and 2nd St.) was another example of how sometimes (though becoming more frequent lately) I don't always understand my own stories, but thank goodness my audience usually does and they will tell me right away. Sometimes I feel that I am adjusting to what they are listening to and feeling — rather than they adjusting to what I'm saying and feeling.

Recently, during public readings, I have felt my stories changing before my eyes as I read — or at least somewhere in midstream I begin to discover, for the first time, what my story is really about by reading it to an audience — by the way an audience listens. It is always so palpable to me the way an audience listens.

When I first wrote this story I thought it was pretty funny that this poor guy would think the bank teller — with whose face he is obsessed — would send him a message hidden between the dots of an ellipsis in what otherwise seems to be a formal letter sent by her from the bank. It's absurd, it's pathetic, but it is funny isn't it? Well, I think yes and no. It's funny strange yes, but funny ha ha? I don't think so.

Of course everything nowadays would point to my main character being psychotic and we do not laugh at psychotics as much as we used to — psychotics are no longer funny or symbolic or mad in a wonderful Dostoyevskian kind of way, but really they are people with an illness for which we insist they seek medication. Perhaps if my bank guy was on medication he wouldn't be so obsessed about the teller — or perhaps never even imagined her — his brain would be too dulled to imagine the ellipsis — he would remember his job and know he had to be on time. In other words, if he stays on his medication there goes the story.

We want psychotics — the mentally ill — to be all right, to be like us — and as far as we go — as far as this world goes these days — is it really that unlikely that we may become like them ourselves — that our identification as unconscious as it may be — has become much stronger with the dispossessed and the oppressed and the mentally ill and how thin that line feels between us and them?

There used to be much more of a distinct separation and distance between the reader and the mad men and women of literature but maybe not so much anymore that now anyone anytime anywhere seems subject to the worst afflictions mental or physical imaginable.

I used to imagine the inmates of a mental facility (or insane asylum we used to call it) as nothing else but the manifestations of our worst nightmares — it would frighten me just to see their vague shadows behind the bars of their windows — and now I sit next to many of them on the subway.

My poor obsessed character is absurd — in the literary sense — he lives in an absurd Kafkaesque world, but as absurdity has become more and more real for us these days we tend to take absurd characters more seriously and wish secretly that they might come out all right in the end and that the author might put them on medication, make them productive members of society rather than have them live permanently in their delusions or let's say between the eyes of a pet goldfish and sometimes as well that fine line between fiction and reality becomes as murky as an unfiltered fish tank.

I have to admit I did find myself not laughing but crying, in particular at the end when the young man finds his ellipsis and crawls inside — inside his head — forever — to live or die with his delusions intact.

Indeed, I started to feel for this character as I had never felt for him before, not for one minute while writing or revising this story. This man was a caricature, a representational delusional feckless absurdity that I would never connect myself with though he was obviously living inside me the whole time. And now this audience had brought him out of me, alive, palpable, pathetic, terrifying and terrified — Okay, fine — but then what can I do for him? I have no medicine. I have no cure. I'm just the author. I can create him but after that all I can do is put him out there — in the tragic and uncertain world in which he must live — watch him struggle day and night with his demons — and then cry for him.

Chapter 17

MOSQUITOES

The reader tonight has arrived 40 minutes late. The person he's reading with, my friend Ernest, has been waiting a long time and starts to get a little nervous because the person he's reading with has never been here before. The reading is in a place called The Hut which is in the backyard of the house owned by my neighbors, Rose and Daniel, who are hosting this reading and providing free food and wine. I notice Daniel keeps whisking away empty bottles of wine three at a time, sticking a finger into each one and then bringing back new ones. He and his wife are amazingly patient. I'm pissed because I wanted to get home at a decent hour and watch TV with my family, which relaxes me, but the window of decent hours is quickly diminishing.

Ernest's co-reader arrives. I had thought he was a male but Ernest tells me that's changed recently and not to be surprised when she shows up. Her name used to be Thomas but now it's Terry. When she does finally show up we still mill around a while and now I can see Ernest getting a bit antsy. "Should we go inside?" Rose asks. "Yes," Ernest and everyone else agrees. "Let's."

Once inside the crowd kind of sits and doesn't sit. It takes a while for everyone to get settled.

This might be because ironically too many people know each other. It's kind of an incestuous group, a little out of control. I ask Rose if I should bring my glass of wine into The Hut and she says, "Yes, you definitely should. By all means you should." So I place it on the empty seat next to me and I notice the woman behind and to the right of me has the same idea. Then my friend   introduces Terry. She wears a blonde wig, red lipstick, high heels, breasts and edits a poetry magazine which no one can pronounce. She tells Ernest he can call it whatever he wants and then thinks better of it. "Well maybe that's not such a good idea," she says. She comes up with a stack of what she calls Prose Poems. "So," she says. "I have a half hour. Lets see," and proceeds to read, looking at her watch every 30 seconds or so. A mosquito begins to buzz in my ear maybe every 10 seconds or so. Sometimes Terry looks at her watch at the same time she is reading and though I know it's rude for an audience member to look at her watch, I wonder if it works the other way around. What I'm a little offended about is that she doesn't seem to respect her poems very much not just sticking a watch in their face but kind of tossing the poem away before even reading the last line. Sometimes she reads the wrong or an older version of a poem and halfway through she stops and clutches her chest as if she suddenly sees an older version of herself as well. Then she thumbs through her stack of poems until she finds the new version and begins again. She seems a little new at this but the audience seems to enjoy every move, every sound, every self — interruption she makes. The mosquito still buzzes around my ear. "Ok," Terry says looking at her watch again, "That's 10 minutes. So I have 20 more. Let's see." I wave hopelessly at the mosquito or rather the sound of it, that insistent buzzing those continual attempts to land on or in my ear which my blind waving seems to discourage for only a brief moment. Then Terry begins to read another poem and in the middle of it the phone in her giant red purse begins to ring. In mid line she goes over and looks at it. "It's Martin," she says, "He probably wants to tell me he's going to be late." The audience or at least those who know her and Martin, which seems to be most of them, laugh. Then she starts the poem where she left off. She looks at her watch. She seems so afraid of time running away from her or maybe that it's not running away fast enough. When she finishes her poem, Rose says, "Maybe your friend is trying to get in the house. I locked the door. Would you like me to go see if he's still waiting out there?" The poet and the audience seem very agreeable to the idea. It's a very agreeable audience. I feel that if she just stood there farting for a half hour they would be fine with it. I feel like getting up and going out for more wine. I feel like calling up the New Christy Minstrels and asking them to come down for some wine. What the fuck? Now was the very witching hour of the night when I could do such things, the earth would quake upon it, but what good would that do if this audience would be fine with it?

So Ernest's co-reader stops her reading and waits patiently for Martin to arrive. The mosquito keeps buzzing in my ear. I constantly swat at it but it doesn't do any good. It comes back at me with more determination than ever. Then Martin arrives with another friend. The poet begins again and as she shuffles through her papers trying to find another poem to read, she keeps saying, "No, no, no," as if each poem is a part of her former self.

Someone from behind taps me on the shoulder. It's Martin, a man with black framed glasses and an English accent. He says he notices the mosquito that keeps flying around my ear and would I mind if he tried to catch it. He says he's always been very good at catching mosquitoes in mid air. "Sure," I tell him. "Knock yourself out." Terry has begun to read again. When she finishes someone suggests we take a break.

Rose agrees and people go out to drink more wine. After we return, Terry, whose time apparently is now up, introduces my friend who seems to take a long time to find a poem to read, but the moment he does, someone taps me on the shoulder again. It's Martin and this time he doesn't say a word but just opens his hand where a dead, not to mention, crushed mosquito lies. "Thanks," I whisper. I turn around again. I listen to my friend who writes about the migratory habits of the arctic tern but I can't help think instead about that dead crushed mosquito in Martin's hand. Something feels wrong. What strange thrill did I spawn, did I sanction, by allowing him to kill the — no my — my own mosquito? It's a weird feeling and I don't like it. After all if a mosquito is bothering you, shouldn't you be the one to kill it? I think of it dead in his hand.

Then our hostess Rose says, "Hey everyone, let's take a break and then we'll start over again."

I think she meant "again," not "over again". I also thinks she wants more wine and doesn't want to wait till the end of the reading. Ernest, who had been looking for quite a while for another poem to read, agrees. "Yes, let's," he says. At this rate, I think, we might be here all night. Ernest's friend stands in a corner with Martin and his friend, laughing, at times clutching her chest, and in general basking in the glory of her miraculous transformation. Why am I jealous? Would I too like to be a woman? I don't really feel like it. At least not at the moment but how wonderful I think to make such a commitment, to make some irrevocable choice, to clutch at your chest after so many years of dissatisfaction and to find the ripe, fleshy burgeoning of hope. In the darkness I suddenly like everyone and feel somehow I belong. I see Martin grabbing mosquitoes in midair and grow fond of him and his foolishness and forgive him right away for his earlier violations of the air space around my ears. Everyone drinks wine and eats olives and puts the pits everywhere and anywhere; it is truly an orgy of olive pits. Daniel keeps whisking bottles away with his three fingers and bringing more back like a tall lanky Bacchus drunkening his thankful guests. And Rose. How beautiful she is, how happy she seems to have these people drinking and eating and listening to poetry in her home. Perhaps she never wants it to end and plans on having a break after every one of Ernest's poems.

When we return to The Hut I sit right in front of Martin again and wait, wait for Ernest to find a poem to read, wait for the buzz of another mosquito. Then Terry's phone rings. It's her friend Tony. He's late. He got lost. Rose goes out to get him. Ernest says he's found a poem. Then he looks up and notices everyone is gone. Except me. Then he leaves to get more wine.

I have enough I tell him and sit where I am. Alone. A mosquito buzzes in my ear. I do not swat it away. The more it buzzes the more it sounds like a poem. I hear the buzzing also of people's voices outside. I imagine I am sitting along the shore of a river in 12th Century China where there are many mosquitoes and many voices and sometimes they would even change places with each other to just see what it would be like and then they would write about it, carefully, deliberately, as if their very lives depended on it.

CPSIA information can be obtained
at www.ICGtesting.com
Printed in the USA
FSHW012317090521
81195FS

9 780983 666899